Behind Silent Eyes

THE SECRETS WITHIN

by Ianū Tebetrū

DORRANCE
PUBLISHING CO
EST. 1920
PITTSBURGH, PENNSYLVANIA 15238

Dorrance Publishing Co
585 Alpha Drive
Suite 103
Pittsburgh, PA 15238
Visit our website at *www.dorrancebookstore.com*

ISBN: 979-8-8868-3047-7
eISBN: 979-8-8868-3911-1

Behind Silent Eyes

THE SECRETS WITHIN

"Today I Let You Go"

AT ONE POINT, YOU USED TO BE MY BEST FRIEND, MY FANTASY, MY safety, and today I threw you away like a needle that would no longer function because there were no other spots to shoot up and take me away to a world, my illusion of what I called home. What I call my endless dreams that I created because I did not want to deal with reality, even though the true battles were being presented in front of me. You made me believe that hurting myself and the ones that I loved were okay. Because as long as I could have you and not have to deal with the cry and hurt and the pain I allowed within myself, I allowed myself to take the best of others, even if it were hurting the ones that I loved and held close.

There were times I wanted to run away from you. I no longer wanted you in my life. I saw what you were doing to my friends and loved ones. You were my weakness when I did not have anyone else to turn to, because they could not do it anymore. You took me to what I thought was reality to only be turned into illusions, a myth that I had created in my mind believing that it was all real, yet being called crazy.

Today I am letting you go, you are a drug I no longer want in my life. You cheated and you lied. I allowed you to take every aspect of my life and who I was. I allowed you to take me out of reality and what was really important to me. Today, I throw you away and walk away and never look back. Today I don't need you in my life; yes, there may be days that you will always be in the back of my mind at times, but they are those little reminders that where I am today is better than where I was then. That I have control of my life more than the years we spent together.

Today I let you go, not because I have to, but because I want to do something different with my life. Today I want to stand up for myself and be honest with myself, and not to have to cheat myself or the ones I love. Today I say thank you for letting me experience what I had to and what I had to go through; because of you, I am where I am and stronger than I ever have been in my life. Today I celebrate my freedom more than I ever have, and I don't have to hide anymore. I can take the mask off my face and throw it away along with a new me, but a new tomorrow.

Life has a funny way of working itself out, even at the least when we expect it, and at the same time it takes some short of impact in our lives, sometimes small and others big, not knowing the meaning or understanding of life itself, but knowing that what comes our way we get to chose to walk through them and experience them, then other times... sometimes we don't have a choice in the decisions in what we feel or want to express or how certain things should be controlled. It has been twenty years since I have really told my story, and what really happened for the first seven years of my life in the Romanian Orphanage, and why I could not tell anyone what really happened, how I let dark memories and secrets lead me to a path of webs of drug addictions, and battling suicide attempts over the fifteen years. The secrets and memories that also affected me, even when I got adopted and came into the U.S., and why my adopted parents had given me back to the state after only really living with them a short time. The only way that I knew I was going to overcome my nightmares and fears was to write my stories, to tell people what really happened, why even the ones that were adopted from the Romanian orphanage can't still talk about it to this day, and why it affected them and still does to this day. The only way that I knew to move on and not let a memory affect my life and what I could become was to tell my story before it became too late and I had let a nightmare take the best of me. Today I celebrate three years of being clean from drug addictions, and a year clean from thoughts of suicide. It was not until last month that I had decided to write my book. At one point, I wrote a three hundred-page manuscript on my life. Out of fear of people seeing my secrets and dark memories, I burned the manuscript, never to talk about it or bring it up again; that was five years ago. I then decided to come out and tell my stories on how I have overcome my battles of suicide and drug addiction. What I am doing is different and why people need to hear my story, how I let dark paths affect me for more than fifteen years, to be free and what I did differently.

As many of you may have remembered, between the early 80's and mid 90's, 20/20 and many other tv networks did stories on Romanian orphanages:

how the children were treated and what we went through, at least what they saw, but along with my adopted parents, many of other adopted parents that had rescued these children did not have the full understanding of what we went through. The only ones that truly knew were the ones that had to go through it and live it behind closed doors. It had been March 31, 1991 that my dreams of coming to America and being adopted by an American family had finally come true; at the time I was seven years old. I had landed at the Denver Colorado Airport to be greeted by my new faces, family that was going to be in my life. I had remembered being so scared and not knowing what to expect because this was my first time in a whole new world that I had heard about in the orphanage, and after seven years of nightmare, I was finally free and was going to have the family and love that I had always dreamed, an ever-ending story if you call it, or at least that's what my adopted parents had thought. I had spent seven years in an orphanage where I could not be picked up, nurtured, or get any of the other treatments that any child should get; instead I was neglected, abused, torchbearer, along with other things that still haunt me to this day.

> "Don't let people, places and things get the best of your world, be proud and stand up and fight for who and what you are. Wearing a mask makes you weak, being your true inner self is just a stepping stone to being the person you're meant to be, not what others think you should be labeled as." Never be scared to express your thoughts and your feelings. Stand up and fight for who and what you can become; embrace today and let yesterday go as it is done and over with. Don't let tomorrow's worries get the best of your emotions, for it has not arrived. Live and breathe for today, and enjoy and embrace it to the fullest as if it was your last (poem1).

I remember the night that I had landed at the Denver Colorado Airport. I know that I was scared and not sure what to think of; I had been greeted by what would be my new family, and the only thing that I could remember was that my dreams had come true. I found myself waving a little American flag in my hands saying, "America." After spending some time at the airport and meeting my new cousins and grandparents, we had gone to what would be my very first real home that I was going to be living in. I remember entering the house to be approached by two dogs that my parents had at the time, one being a German shepherd named Patty and the other one named Willy. I had been scared of them and ran the other way because of the things I had experienced and seen in the orphanage, so I had been very scared of dogs. Once I was calmed down and the dogs were taken somewhere else, I was then taken to what would be pretty much my own room. At that time, I was sharing the room with my new little sister who was less than a year old and had also been adopted from Romania from a different family. We had gotten adopted at the same time and brought over. In the room on one side of the wall, I had my bed with gifts that my new adopted parents had gotten for me, new clothes and pants and shoes, and new toys, things that I had dreamed of that I had never thought I would get the experience to have. On the other side of the wall near the door of the room was my little sister's crib, and if I am correct, one side of the wall had been painted with different animals and what not.

Learning English was very new for me, and I had no understanding of it, so I spent some years at home being taught English and certain basic things, to get me ready for going to public school. At the same time I was taught right from wrong. My adopted parents had things coming to them that they had not expected. I had found myself walking into people's homes due to not knowing any better; I had acted out a lot when I was trying to be disciplined. I had tried going to public school after a couple of years of being in the U.S, which did not last long. I was convinced that my adopted parents had placed in into a different orphanage, seeing other kids there, so it freaked me out. I had acted up a lot, so my first time of going to school did not last as long as my adopted parents had figured. So in the meantime, I had my adopted mother teach me the basic things I needed to know and discipline, but each time I was tried to be taught from right and wrong or any type of education, I had lashed out. Every time that my adopted parents tried to bond with me, I would push away and act out, lash out, and get out of control. I had found myself trying to get back into school after a while, only to be being kicked out for stomping on a teacher's foot and slapping her against the face for her picking me up and trying to comfort me. I did not have good relationships with women; it had to do a lot with what they did to me in the orphanage, so any woman trying to comfort me was more of a threat to me that they did not understand. Instead, they thought I lashed out for no reason and there was no true understanding as to why my behavior was the way it was. I was expelled from school and was home again. I had problems with authority and stealing mail from people's mailboxes. I stole wallets at one point, and had acted out a lot because I had no idea what was right or wrong. I did not have discipline the proper way that I should have, so whatever I thought I was doing was no harm, and instead it was doing harm to the loved ones around me.

I had only lived with my adopted parents until I was 12 years old. You see, it was my "out of control behavior," that had me sent to different therapist sand group homes. My adopted father did the best that he could and tried to love the way that he could and knew how, but I think more of his lashing out and hitting me and what I called abuse as a child. There were times that man would pick me up out of anger and slam me against a wall, yelling or slapping me to where blood would come out of my nose. There were times I went to school with dry blood on my face and being asked what happened, I had made excuses because of the fear that if I told what would happen to me; I had lied in that family, manipulated, and did not want to work on a loving bonding relationship, what I had wanted most and what they did not realize, was that I did not want them in my life. I did not want them as my parents, and I was going to do whatever it took not to be near them. The fear, the what if's and what would happen the next day, the fear of going to sleep only to cover myself with a blanket hoping to make the memories and thoughts go away. I had done things and acted out of anger. I had decided one summer to start my parents' property on fire. My excuse was that there was a person driving by and had flicked his butt on our property, and it started on fire and almost burned my adopted father's shed that he had built. I had started playing matches in almost 100 degree weather. I had done it because in the summertime, I got up early and was pretty much pushed out the door and locked out until my adopted father got home from work ,because his wife could not deal with me for whatever reason, so she could have cared less what had happened to me. When lunch came around I was called by name, and if she were in the mood, I could eat inside then, would have to go right back outside, but if she were in her bitchy mood, then it was put the food outside and lock the door, so I had done things like start fires, and act out because of the way that I was being treated. I wanted love, not neglect and abuse from two parents that had allowed it at the same time turning their heads, looking the other way, as if nothing had happened and that I had been the fucked up one, that I was the one that needed help. When in reality, they had not been prepared to take what they so craved to have to be placed into their hands, for them only to crush and throw away and to be forgotten.

My adopted parents had tried sending me to a therapist and nothing was seeming to help; instead, it was tearing a family apart, only leaving my adopted parents with one choice and that was to give me to the state where then I could be taken care of by another family. I had been taken to a group home in Colorado that was called the "Willy Ranch." It was a little bit over five acres, had Stalin horses, chicken, goats, and donkeys. More like a little mini farm. The house had three bedrooms upstairs and downstairs had two. The three rooms were occupied, one by me and at that time, a seven-year-old child. I had been twelve at the time; next door to me was another teenage boy, no more than fifteen at the time. He was the only one that had his own room and was told that no one could ever share a room with him or ever enter his room, and that he was a sex offender. I was not really sure on the story of the little guy that I had to share a room with; all I knew was that his name was Austin. He had only shared a room with me the first four months I was there, then he had left and had gone somewhere else, so for many months I had my own room, which to me I would prefer.

I had spent a year with this group home. I had spent my year loading and unloading hay bales on a trailer and driving them to odd places to unload them. When we were not doing that, it was always working on the farm, whether it was shoveling manure or getting milk from the goats; that was the only type of milk that we drank. I had spent the summer taking private school lessons, and then when the school year had come around, I was allowed to go to public schools, which was nice for me because it was a way to meet new friends and not feel trapped where I was. I had spent my time either in school or at the group home; that had been my social life. At night, we had security alarms on our windows and doors, that way if anyone tried to get out of their bedroom door or windows, then not only would the authority know, but also the foster parents. The foster dad was Rod, and the wife was Shelly. Rod was an odd character, always seemed to stick to himself, he had to be about an even six feet, about 160 pounds, with thick black curly hair, but even then, I am not sure if it were all nature curly. His hair seemed always to be all over the place. When we talked or hung out, he had a soft side of him, a humble side of him, and when he needed to be stern, then he would when the appropriate time came. I don't ever recall getting into any type of arguments with him. His wife, on the other, had been an odd relationship; I had never been attached to her nor really took the time to understand her. She was not your average woman; she was a firm Christian woman, hard worker, and never was afraid to get dirty. She had scars all over her face and arms, as if there were stories to be told on her life journey. She had been about 5'8 and about 140 pounds, with thick blond hair that at times was messy as well. She had always worn torn clothes while working; I had never seen any of them dress fancy or nice. While the year that I was in with the state I had seen a councilor by the name of Carol. She was an older woman, in her forties at that time. I had remembered that I would see her several times a week to work on my anger issues and on my past childhood Romanian years of anger and resentment. I had been wrapped up in the pig in a blanket; I remember hating it and not liking it, it always was to hot and made me feel uncomfortable to the point where I did not want to do anything but get out, not to mention I had no desire to go back to my past and relive it and tell it. But I knew that the only way they were going to stop and I was going to go back home, was to tell them what they wanted to hear, and I told them what I could handle and what felt safe at that time to share. The more I had been forced to relive my life in the orphanage, the more I became angry and wanted to shut down. I did not want to have to relive the feeling and they were not understanding as much as they thought that it was helping me, when really, I was building more of a brick wall up every time and it did not make it any better when they were women therapists. I did not have good relationships with the women staff that took care of me for seven years and I was making it quite clear to them that I was not having it.

> Life's decisions are the paths we make and choose along
> the way, sometimes good and sometimes bad, others
> having a true understanding of the paths we were on,
> and others leaving us at a dead end at times, only leaving

us at not having a full understanding of who we are or can become. We sometimes let our pride and emotions get the best of us, some only to hide away from the world because they are told they will never amount to anything nor themselves to be left with scars of endless tears of emotions. We learn to fight our own battles to discover what our meaning is to life and who we really are. It's then that when we get to feel, we express, and when we express, not only are voices heard, but then we become freer within ourselves (poem2).

A year had gone by, and I yet again was united with my adopted family, and I got to go back home. It was supposed to be a new start and that things would be okay and normal, and that we could all have a healthy life; well, at least that's what we were all hoping for. Instead of my behavior improving, it got out of hand, and at times, out of control. I was then again sent to a different therapist to try and work on the underlying issue that I was having and the hopes that I could be somewhat "Fixed and Cured," when really things turned south. I had seen a male therapist in Evergreen Colorado by the name of Dr Neail. The first male therapist I had seen, being that my adopted parents had felt that it would be best for me to try a male therapist rather than a family. I can't tell you that I remember much about him, although every time I went to see him and we talked and worked together, I could always smell cigarettes on his breath and clothes, and the more I saw him and talked to him, the more I started to open up slowly and started to work on issues, one step at a time. I remember starting to feel comfortable telling him certain things that I knew I could try and tell. There was one thing that he wanted to know and what had happened; I had remembered that I had been uncomfortable about the question he had asked me and wanted me to share and tell of what had happened that day, and what I had remembered. Yet at the same time, there was a calm little feeling in me that felt at ease. I looked at him and started off to say...

It had been a warm sunny day that day, a light breeze in the air. You could hear children running around, laughing and playing on the two seat wings, and other kids throwing sticks at the apple tree to get apples. I had been playing with two of my friends that day, running around and chasing each other like any other kids would, when all of a sudden, I had been approached by a gentleman that had been 6'0. He had dark brown, short hair that was clean and cut. His blue eyes were covered with glasses that covered his face. He was well-dressed in light brown slacks and a sweatshirt over his dress shirt and tie. He could not have been more than thirty at the time. He had come up to me and kneeled down to me; as I was eye level with him, I could smell a cologne smell that he had on him, it was not an overwhelming smell, but a more of a light, sweet smell. He proceeded to tell me that he was a therapist, he had put it in terms that I could understand, he had told me that he was kind of like a doctor and that he needed to make sure I was healthy, and that I needed to answer some questions. I then agreed by nodding my head and proceeded to follow him inside the orphanage down the dark hall all the way to the end of the building where then we walked into a room that had no window, had a lamp in a corner that had dimmed the room. There was a desk with a chair facing the door, and a small, two-seater couch that had been sitting up against the left side of the room against the wall. Beside the couch, there was a small chair that he had moved in front of the desk. He then looked at me with a smile on his face, patting the chair, telling me that it was okay, that there was nothing to worry about, and that he just needed to ask me some questions, and that it would not take long our first time. He had then proceeded to tell me that we were going to be meeting a few times out of the month. I then sat in the chair as I was facing him. He had folders of some sorts and a briefcase that had been almost on the edge of the office table. He had a notepad and a pen that he had previous notes in, and then had looked at me and asked if I were ready to answer some questions. I looked at him and nodded. I remembered being scared. Not sure what to expect or what was going to come out of this, all I knew was that he seemed to be nice and non-threatening. He had asked how I was feeling and if I were okay; I responded by nodding my head again to a yes answer. He looked at me with a smile, and he got out of his seat, came over, and kneeled in front of me. As he did, I jumped a little and he saw that I had gotten used to being hit for no reason at times, and so I did not trust anyone. He had noticed and proceeded to say that there was nothing to be scared of, that whatever was talked about would never leave the room, and that I could trust him.

He passed for a few minutes looking at me, then stood up and looked down at me and said, "Let's continue this for the next several days. Does that sound okay?" I replied yes. He then walked to the door and opened it, and told me that I was welcome to go back outside and play with my friends. Without even thinking or blinking an eye, I ran out of the room. I can remember he seemed to be a nice person, but there was something about him that did not feel right, a feeling that was not settling well with my stomach. I had gone outside to go play with my friends without saying anything and going back to what we were doing; several children had run to me and asked what had happened. I had told them nothing and they left it at that. Sometimes we thought it was better not to talk about some of the things that have happened to us, because if we did and the staff found out, a lot of the times the consequences were worse and they were things that we did not want to go through. Being locked up in the cages and being treated like animals and left in there for days.

Like so many children that go through some type of trauma, they don't want to have to relive it nor talk about it. I had stopped and told him that I did not want to talk about it anymore, that I did not want to think about it anymore, the more I had thought about it and had flashbacks, the more I had become sick inside only to want to throw up the memories. He had looked at me to tell me that it was fine and that we could stop for the day, and hopefully pick up the next time we were going to see each other, I had remembered telling him that I did not want to talk about it anymore, and that it was too hard for me, he had told me that if I did not talk about them and get them out and work on the issues, then I was going to be affected by them for the rest of my life, and that if I wanted a healthy life with a healthy family, that then I would need to work on the issues. Before I had left that day, he had told me and my adopted mother that he felt it would be best if once or twice a week I laid across her lap while she held me, like a mother would hold their newborn, and talk about my day and talk about our feelings. I know for me it was something that I was not excited about, something that was hard for me; it had been that my adopted mother and I had not had the greatest start as far as a relationship since I was adopted and brought into the United States. I remember it not lasting long; I know that for me it had been very uneasy and something that I was not ready to fully commit to. I had woman trust issues, so it was hard to try and express feelings to a mother, let alone try to work on resolved issues that were hidden for so many years. I recall not seeing Dr. Neail for more than a couple of months of treatment; my behavior there for a while was good and getting the way that it should have been. But there were still things there that were not focused on nor taken care of. I was working on my past in the orphanage but had neglected to work on the relationship with what should have been my adopted mother, instead only to be looked upon as a person in my life that was trying to the best that they knew how and could. While I was home and still working with Dr. Neil, and also things with my adopted mother that Dr. Neil had assigned us, I can remember it being very difficult for me. I had a hard time understanding my feelings, and had a hard time understanding why I was trying to be forced to be loved. There had been so many times that I pushed away from my adopted mother, I did not know how to love or to bond, and I did not have a good relationship with the woman in the orphanage, and the relationship that I my adopted mother and I had was already strained since I had gotten adopted. I had seemed to adapt more to my adopted father than her. I had struggled to know who I was and what I was, why I was feeling the way that I was. They say that children should feel safe and comfortable to share their feelings and thoughts with their parents; in my case it was not that. I had remembered the first time that I tried to commit suicide. I had been very young at that time; I can't tell you how I even knew the word suicide, but I knew that I wanted to be done and not feel the way that I was feeling anymore. You see, my adopted father and I had what I would call "strained unknown emotions." I can't say that my adopted father really knew how to raise children nor was he prepared for what he was going to be faced with and have to deal with for the rest of his life.

> "Today I give thanks for letting me experience the better side of who I am today and what more I can become tomorrow. Today I give thanks to the support that surrounds my everyday struggles and the faith to walk on a better path of tomorrow and not steer to paths of illusions but the paths of faith and courage to endless possibilities. Today I give thanks for the joy in my life and not the past of yesterday's sorrowful memories. Today I give thanks for giving me wings to fly, to experience, to feel and to understand the better side of not only me.. but the path of what is meant to be" (poem 3).

I had thought that when I got adopted into this American family, that I would be safe, that the things that happened to me in the orphanage would never happen to me again, and that I would be safe and loved the way that I have always wanted to and dreamed of. My trying to attempt suicide at the age of 14 started when I could no longer take the heating from my adopted father. There were times I was scared that man was going to beat me to the point that I was not going to make it. I never had an understanding for the way that he would hit me, slap me across the face, or sometimes even pick me up, then slam me up against a wall, only to yell at me and make me feel as though it was all my fault. I can remember that his hitting started when I was in fifth grade. There were several days out of the week that I would show up to school with bloody noses because he would get upset about something in the morning before I went to school, and I would be found at times to be slapped so hard that blood would come out of my nose. After yelling, he would clean it off before I would walk down the road to go to school and pretend as nothing happened, but only feeling scared and not knowing what to do, I did not feel safe to talk to them, nor did I feel safe to come home. As time went by, the family was being torn apart worse than the first time; my adopted father's beating me got more out of control. Soon CPS and Child Services got involved because the school would see dry blood on my nose, and when asked, I was too scared to tell the truth because if I did, then he may hurt me. I had tried running away two times because of the fact that I could not do it anymore and I no longer wanted this family. My relationship with my adopted mother was not any better; if anything, between the both of us, it was like a scab that would try to heal, but it would just be picked at to the point that it got infected and you ended up needing serious treatments.

> "Dear God...
> I thank you for the strength you gave me to become
> stronger in my most weakest moments and allowing me
> to become stronger within myself and what I can be-
> come. Dear God, make me a bird.. So that I may ex-
> pand my wings and fly into the sunset and let dreams
> become endless possibilities (poem 4).

I had remembered always wanting a family more than anything. I had craved a love and a touch from a mother and a father, but not knowing how, and not going through the healthy way was very hard for me to grasp, even when I tried to have a relationship with my adopted mother. There was a time that I really wanted to try and make something work with her, even though I was scared and trying to understand and figure out what I was feeling, and why, until the day that she had devastated me and tore my heart out, that made me not even want to work on a relationship with her let alone even try. You see, I had wanted the handheld CD player that came out at the time; they were the big, square-looking ones, and they were the new hip thing, everyone had them, and I wanted one. I then approached my adopted father to tell him that I really wanted this CD player. I knew that he was not just going to give me the money and I could go get it and everything would be fine. His way at times was you had to work it to earn what you wanted, so he had told me that for every thorn that I picked, I would get 25 cents a head, and I could save up that money to get what I wanted, so I did. I had spent the summer picking thorns and placing them into grocery bags. Every night when my adopted father came home, I would have bags full of them, and he would check how many I had in each bag and pay me based on that. At the end of the summer, I was able to get myself not only the CD player, but also several CDs, because I had extra money left over. And it was perfect because it was just the beginning of a new school year and since I had a long walk to the school bus, then I could have a listen to music on the way, well... at least that's what I had thought. Both of my parents had agreed that they wanted me only to have the CD player at the house, and I was not to take it and listen to it while walking to the bus or even school. I had remembered being upset; I had worked hard for this to only find out that I could only listen to it at home or if I were going with them to places. After arguing and not getting anywhere, I had given up on the fact of trying to convince them to let to me take the CD player, but I was not giving up on the fact of being able to still use it when I wanted. So I found myself sneaking the CD player in my backpack or into my clothes where it could not be seen, and then when I got away from the house where then I knew I could not be seen for sure, and I knew I was in the clear, then I would pull my it out and start to listen to music. I had done it for a while, thinking that I was getting away with it, until one day I had come home to get confronted on the issue by my adopted mother telling me that she did not see it in the room, and that she was looking for it and had asked where it was. I had pulled it out and gave it to her, upset and knowing that it was going to be taken away. She then told me that I would be dealing with the issue with my father when he got home from work. When he arrived home, he had walked into my room with the CD player in his hands and had looked at me and asked why I had taken the CD player to school knowing that I was not supposed to. I had responded that I wanted to listen to music while walking to the bus stop; after all, walking to the bus stop was a mile away, and I had proceeded to tell him that I liked to listen to it on the bus, and that when I am in school I put it away. He had told me that it was still not right to do what I did. I can't recall as to what the final decision was, but I remembered that I got my CD player back and I had been very excited about that. I had discovered that music was something that helped me cope with my thoughts and feelings. I had decided to take the CD player again with me the next morning to school, knowing that I was not supposed to. I had made it to my bus and got on and had several other stops we were to make before I was to go to school, and I thought I had gotten away without anyone noticing that the C player was not in my room. While showing my friend my CD player and listening to music, the bus was just about to leave when it stopped again, and the door opened. There was my adopted mother there looking for me. My heart sunk and started to beat as I knew what the reason for her to stop the bus was. I quickly gave my CD player to what was my best friend at the time, told him to hold on to it, and that when I got to school, I would grab it from him. I then grabbed my things and got off the bus; it then pulled away and she had asked where the CD player was. I had told her that one of my friends had it. We had gotten into an argument, she demanded that I got into the car, and I had told her no. She then proceeded to tell me that she was going to call my father. My heart sank even more because he was one man I was even more scared of, but I still fought and had said no. Somehow I decided to give in until she had told me that we were going home and that I was not going back to school. I had then opened the door as she was driving as she hit her brakes, and I got out. She was screaming for me to get back in the car. I had yelled back to tell her no and that I did not want to go home and be around her, and that I wanted to go to school and that I hated her. After more yelling, I finally got into the car; I had known I was not going to win; it was not the yelling and screaming that affected me. It had been what she had told me on the way home, something that no young child should ever have to hear. She had looked at me and told me, "If it weren't for your father, I would dump your sorry ass back into that orphanage and leave you there to rot and die." That's when I had shut down all feelings and emotions to her; my heart had been broken and torn. She then had told me that she did not want to deal with me, that she was going to take me back to school, and that my father could deal with me when I got home. I had told her that I was not going to come home nor did I want to. She then had told me that I was just going to stay home. I then had told her that I was just going to run away and that it did not matter, I had no longer wanted to be near them or apart of their lives. She had made up her mind to drive me to school, still fighting and yelling back and forth all the way to the school, as she was demanding that I go into the school, grab the CD player, and bring it to her, or she would do it. I guess that someone had seen us or heard us fighting, because once I got the CD player from my friend and returned it to my adopted mother only to slam the door on her face as she was talking, at that point, she was dead to me, and I did not give a darn about her and her feelings. Once I got into my first class, I didn't even have five minutes to sit down before I had the councilor of the school open the door and ask for me. I had grabbed my things and had walked to the class door where she was waiting for me. She had closed the door behind her and we started walking towards her office; while we were doing so, she had mentioned that a staff had seen and heard some of the arguments outside and had seen that I had been distracted, and wanted to know if everything had been okay, and most importantly, if I had been okay. We had gotten into her office, and I had explained to her what had happened and how it happened, and the fact that I was too scared to go home, and that there was no way that I was going to go home nor did I have the intention.

After talking for a while, I was excused from my regular classes, an hour or two when yet again I had been approached by the school counselor, only to be told that my father was on the phone and that he had wanted to talk to me. I agreed and followed her into her office. I picked up the phone. "Hello?" … other end … "Ian? Are you okay? What happened, and what is going on, and why is your mother crying?" I had told him on the other line of what had happened and what she had said ,and that I was not going to come home, I did not want to come home, and I didn't want to be around her or have anything to do with her. He then had asked me what I was going to do and where I was going to go. I had responded to tell him that it did not matter and that I would figure it out, that maybe I could stay with one of my friends for the weekend, but that there was no way I was going to nor wanted to come home. He then asked me if it would be okay if he came to see me and get me after school. I had remembered being hesitant because of the fear that no matter what, he was going to take me home, and I did not know what was going to be done after that. He had told me that he wanted to get me and that we could talk and figure out something, but we did not have to go home right away. I agreed. I hung up the phone. Once I did that, I was told that I was not going to my regular class that day, but in a quiet room with others where I could work at my own pace and not be distracted or worried. When school got out, I went outside to see that my adopted father was outside waiting for me. I then got into the car, and he had told me that we would go somewhere where we could sit and talk and figure out what was going on. I had been surprised to see that he was so calm about it, suttee, I thought for sure that I was going to get yelled at or beaten again. But instead, he had asked what went on, and what led to how it had come down to this. I had started explaining to him how it happened and what the outcome of it was. As we were talking, we had found ourselves at a quiet park and continued talking about what had happened. I then was asked by my adopted father what I wanted to do; I had told him that there was no way I was going to go home, that I did not want to go home, and I no longer wanted to deal with her. He had told me that we were going to have to go home for a couple of hours, while he made some phone calls and saw where I could be placed. Once I had gone home, I was told to hang out in my room and that he was going to start making calls. Hours had gone by and it started getting dark; when my hopes of leaving had come to a fail, the door had opened and there was my adopted father to tell me that there was nothing that could be done tonight, but that the next day I would be going to stay at a temporary group home in our town for the weekend, then they would go from there. I had been upset that I could not leave that night, but was more anxious for tomorrow to come. I had not wanted to be in the same house as her. I did not want to be close to her, nor have anything to do with her. The next day had come. I had been woken up that early morning and was told that I needed to start packing my clothes and things, so I did, and after I was done, my adopted father and I had left for me to go live in my new group home. One the way down, I had remembered looking at him and seeing his body expression, facial expression, as much as he was trying to not show it, but he was scared, upset, confused, and not sure what to do…more of a lost feeling, lost emotions of not knowing how to handle.

It's hard to talk about a man that I once grew to love, a man that I had looked up to for so many years and once called my "hero," a person that I would have fought to the end of the world to be there and support, no matter what it took, and no matter how much I had gotten hurt, how do you tell a story about a man that once made since only to disappear into a world of dark webs and be pushed away for more than nearly 15 years? I can truly say that I love my adopted father as a person, but as a father, as a parent… I can't say that, nor do I feel the same way that I did when I was a child before I was given up to the states. I had remembered the day when I saw him in the orphanage and when I was in the hospital; there was something about him that made me feel right, and he was the father I wanted in my life, the father I wanted to grow to love and be a best friend and son. What would have come my way and if I had known things would have been different? My adopted father is about 5'9 in my option, but I could be wrong, blue eyes, short hair, a mustache; he was a broad man, husky, but not fat, just built, a loving man, a caring man, but at the same time a man with a lot of childhood hurt with his own past family relationship that I still have no understanding of, accepted that he did not have a good strong relationship with his father. He came from a small town to Delmont, South Dakota, and grew up on a farm with hard labor, with a strained relationship with his father and a healthy one with his mother, At the age of 19, he decided to join the military, and from there I have no clue about his life and what he has gone through, I don't know anything about his life, as if he has hid that from the world because it was too much, and he just wanted to try and forget about it. When I came to the U.S., I can say from seven years old to 12 years old, our relationship was a love-hate relationship, and that was on my end more, and how I felt and took it throughout the years. I never had a full understanding of what love was, nor what discipline was, so yeah, I was an out-of-control child that did what I wanted and lied and stole. Without having that for seven years, it was hard to understand why things happened the way they did and how they had to go about it. I don't think that my adopted father truly had the full understanding of what it was going to take to raise a child that had been where I had been for the first seven years of my life. I can truly say that my adopted parents did the best that they knew how, and they wanted that "perfect family," but sometimes life has a funny way of playing, and like the saying goes, "God brings children into parents' life to teach them tolerance."

My adopted father was hard on me for the five years that I had lived with him, and I know he wanted what was best for me. He wanted me to have a good life and make it in the world. I think more he did not want me to have the life that he did with his father, as to why he tried something different, but throughout the years, some of the things I did brought out his father in him when he got mad, when I acted out, or when there was something he did not like. There was yelling, and there was hitting, even at times being thrown up against the wall only to see pure anger in that man's eyes, yet so much hurt and guilt behind his eyes. I know he meant well, and he felt horrible about what he did after he did it. He had seen that he became his own father and he let his feelings get the best of him and his own world. He had let his memories of his childhood past get the best of his world, to the point that it affect him and his world to where it affected me, and the ones that he so tried to love and be there for. My adopted father is what you could call a man of dark secrets, a man that never wanted to share, because the thoughts and feelings got the best of him.

"I thank you for the strength you gave me to become stronger in my moments of weakness at times being faced with unknown decisions. I thank you for allowing tears to not be expressed of sadness but the tears of courage and strength. Today I thank you for not letting temptations get the best of who I am but instead embracing courage and faith allowing me to stay focused on a path of endless opportunities in my life, and not paths of spiering illusions of webs, but to embrace each second and moment I have in my life" (poem 5).

I can still remember and am haunted a lot by the things in ways that he did and affected me. When he would help me on my homework, and if I could not understand or get it right to his satisfaction, there was yelling or there would be hitting. I never knew how to react, but to be scared of him more and more each day. There were times I was scared to talk to him, or days that I did not know how to talk to him, let alone express my feelings to him. I can't recall any family activities that were really good, most of them. There were times he would ask me how it was that I felt about my adopted mother. I think at that point, I had told him what he wanted to hear, based on not wanting to get hurt, when really inside she was dead to me, when inside I did not want to have anything to do with the woman that was in his life, she was not any better, she stood back and might as well have closed her eyes and turned around, not caring and knowing what he was doing to me, not fighting to make things stop and not caring, as if she got enjoyment out of it. She had been jealous of my adopted father's relationship with me, what was there at least. Every time there was a problem or I did not want to deal with her, I would always run to my adopted father. What she did not realize was that I had a bad experience with females in the orphanage, and the things she did behind my adopted father's back were, in my eyes, more fucked up than what my adopted father did; how in the summer ,she would leave me outside all day, in the morning I was pushed outside until my adopted father got home, sometimes no water, and sometimes no shoes, when it was time to eat, she would set the food outside and lock the door, if she were in a good mood, then I could come in and eat then have to be back outside, when I needed to use the bathroom it had to be outside. I had got pushed away from a monster that I grew to hate and no longer wanted in my life; it was not the life I wanted, how she pulled the covers over my adopted father's face to make things were okay, and when he was not, it was a living nightmare, a mother that had let her emotions get the best of her world and her jealousy tear the family away that my adopted father so once craved and wanted more than anything, only leaving him with the hardest decision that he had to make, and that was to let go of the son that he so craved, the son that he so wanted to raise and do what normal parents do. When it was the maid that I looked at, if I tore the family apart, when really, she, the devil within herself, got what she wanted; she had wanted a perfect family, and when she knew she was not going to have it, she was going to do everything in her power to break the family.

It would have been 15 years that I had been pushed away from a family that I so once had craved and wanted, only to be taken away, and lost and broken with false hopes and broken promises. They had pushed not only me away, but their other adopted child away, from their lives when she found out that she had finally got her dreams, and what they had so craved and tried for so long... a new part of a family member had come into their life. This was at the time when I had been placed into my second group home at Mountain State's children's home, where I would have spent my next five years with hardly any interactions with what was supposed to be my family.

The situation being that he had been stuck in the middle of me and her. He had looked at me while we were driving, and he had asked why I did not like Joyce and what was it about her that I did not want to have any part of. Before I could speak, he had reassured me that it was okay to tell him and that he was not going to get upset. My response in return was I did not like her, I did not love her, and I did not want to be around her. He had told me that he loved me, that I was a good kid with a good heart, and that he was sad that it was not working out the way that he had expected it, and that all that he wanted for me was to be happy and do well in life.

We had arrived at our destination, and we both got out as we were greeted by an older lady; she had asked if there were anything that she could help with. I had only a bag for the weekend so there was not much that she could have done. I can't really tell you much about the group home I was at, because I had only been there for the weekend, and most of the time that I was there, I was playing with other kids. The weekend had passed and I was greeted with both of my parents; I was told that there was going to be a different group home that I was going to go to for a longer period, and that it was not going to be far from them, that they would only be in the next town, which was Longmont, Colorado. I had been told on the way down that where I was going to be was going to be on a farm, that there were going to be horses, pigs, and sheep. And that there were going to be many other children there also. I remembered as we were entering the main driveway. Once we had got into the place, we walked into there main building, we were greeted buy one of the counselors and the director of the program to show us around, and show me the new place that I was going to be living in, and that I would be introduced to the proctor parents, and the other children that I would be living with and sharing a room with. Before we had left the main building, we had all gone to a big office room where my adopted parents and me, my new foster parents that would take care of me, and my counselor along, with other people that I had no clue why they were there, and what their part had been in the whole matter.

I could not make sense of what was all going on; all I knew was that this new place where I would be, what would come down the road for me would be something I had not expected. You see, I had it in my mind that I was only going to be there for a year, like I was at my other place, then I would go back home and maybe everything would become the way that it was supposed to and should have been. I did not know that when they said goodbye and left... I did not know that their goodbyes would be a rollercoaster of unknown emotions. I had met my new proctor parents. Her name was Shelly, she was about 5'8, she had thick blond hair, blue eyes, a little bit on the heavy side, but she was beautiful and kind in her way, and the father was maybe about my height, not much taller, but he was more built not from working out, you could just tell the guy had liked outdoors, and always ate the right stuff. But there was something about him that seemed unsettling. There was another part of him that he was hiding. I felt it; I just was not sure what to think about him all the way. Once my adopted parents had left and we said our goodbyes and what not, I was then escorted by my new proctor parents into the new house that I was going to be living in for however long. Once you had walked in, on the left side of you, there was a living room, where there was a couch and TV, a more of a quiet, calm area. On the right side of you, you were greeted by a kitchen, which indeed had been a good sized kitchen, wooden floors all through the kitchen, a table in the middle that really could feed a house of twelve. And then there had been two different hallways, one on the right and the other on the left. There had been two bedrooms and one bathroom on one side, and the same on the other. After being showed around we then were taken into the main living room to talk further as to what was expected in the home, and what my part was, I had been upset to hear that I was not going to be able to see my adopted parents for 90 days. I had also remembered being scared and not sure what to think of it at the time, although knowing a piece in me knew that I was going to be spending the rest of my teen life of going through different group homes. After I said my goodbyes to my parents, it would be the last time I would see them until the 90 days were done. My first month of being there was already a disaster; I could not really tell you how it all started and why it happened, but I remember I had got so upset over something that I had packed my things up and had up them on the front lawn in bags, and some of the bags I had already come with, and out of frustration.

> "When I become strong within myself... I learn to express the better side of who I want to be And not how others see me best fit in their world. When I become strong within myself... I stop allowing bullying in my life and stand for what's right and what I believe in. When I become strong within myself... I stop lying to myself and the people out there that mean the most to me, to take off the mask and show others who and what I can achieve in my life. When I become strong with myself.... I stop trying to force and take control over things that have no matter or are not time to be presented in my life. When I become strong within myself.. I give more thanks to myself and the people around me that believed in what they saw in me" (poem 6).

I had been walking up and down the road, passing the home where I had been living at the time, knowing the rule was that there was no security on the doors or windows, so if we decided to run away, we then would be reported to the cops and then they themselves would deal with the rest, something that I did not want. I am sure at the time I had looked ridiculous, but I had a cane… a certain cane that meant the world to me, you see, it had come from my grandma, it had a dice on the top and the rest was wooden but a blue color.

I had been walking with it and trying to release any anger that I had; there had been something about that cane that made me feel calm and safe, which was why I walked up and down the road with it, until I had given up and gone back inside, and had recited to take whatever punishment came my way. Several months had gone by and I had finally been allowed to visit with my adopted parents, yet still being scared and nervous, I had grown a fear of the both of them, a fear that no one had known about, a fear that had kept me alive, hoping that one day it would change. Once they had arrived at the group home, we were only allowed a couple of hours, so it was then we decided to go out to dinner and talk about what had happened so far and such. I can't really tell you a lot about the day as I was more confused… and what my part had been.

I had remembered that I wanted to go back to where I was at, feelings and flashbacks had come back being faced with them, anger started to grow inside, and I only wanted to hide away from the world and pretend that it was all a dream. I had pretended to make sure that everything seemed to be great, the fear of ever telling them how I really felt, then what more nightmares would come out to play.

I had remembered being dropped off and had a lot on my mind, endless emotions and thoughts. I had been approached by Shelly (Proctor Mother). She had told me that she knew something was wrong, and that if I wanted to talk, that she was there, as well as her husband Rod. I had nodded my head and had thanked her to find myself walking into my room and lying in bed, wanting to talk to someone and express whatever emotion I had, the ones I understood, and the ones that I could not I wanted answered, but only to silence myself and hide because they might hurt me also. I had started to see one of the main therapists that was there on campus; one day a week, I was allowed with my therapist. I had been used to therapists; they all seemed to say the same thing and try to understand my so-called behavior, and why I was the way I was and why I was acting up, why I was scared to let in, and most of all, that all therapists tried to get out of me but with not of a lot of success, was about my memories in the Romanian orphanage, what had really happened those seven years of my life, and why it was something I could never share. It was the first time that I had really told the therapist that my feelings are better written down rather than talking to someone face to face, because then they don't have to see how I become. She then gave me a notebook and told me that I could write anything in there, and that it would only be between me and her, and that no one else would see it or read it. I had agreed to give it a try; I had spent that week and through the next week writing my thoughts and feelings as to how I really had thoughts about my adopted mother and father, along with other emotions that I had had. It was going to be my therapist's first time to see how I had felt, these were issues that I was going to try to work on in a healthier manner.

There was an issue that I still had, my therapist wanted to know about my Romanian life. I had told her that I would share with her what I felt comfortable with, but that I was not going to share things I was not ready to talk about nor even think about. The more that I wrote, the more I grew to find that writing had become my passion, my comfort, my safety. I was not judged. I had gotten another notebook that I was the only one that knew about, and that what I was going to write in there was going to be all of my secrets and thoughts. They were what helped me to try to understand what it was that I was feeling and what was I to become. As I found myself writing more about my life in the orphanage and the memories, dreams then haunted me even more, and at times waking me up to being drenched in sweat, yet thanking God that it was all a dream. I had a notebook and paper right beside my bed, I had been told that any dream I had, I was to write them and share them with my therapist. Some I would, others I kept to myself never to share, but to hope that those memories would stick to the paper and leave the mind. I had found myself being woken up from a nightmare, that the thought of going back to sleep was impossible, so instead I chose to write what it was that I had flashbacks of and what memories were haunting me.

The cages were small and smelly, and at times, very packed and cramped with naked, helpless orphans. We were left in there for hours, sometimes days, with very little or no food or water; more than half of us were tied up to pulls, we had some kind of hard string, or top or even a ripped bed sheet, that would be tied around our wrists so tightly that sometime our hands would turn different colors. It even got to the point where the skin would start to rot and you could start seeing bones. We screamed because the pain was too much; for every scream, there was the hitting and beating, being told that we are worthless pieces of shit, and that if we did not shut up and listen, that we would be beaten to death and fed to the dogs. When we heard them always bringing up the dogs, that's when we knew that we had to lay there and take the pain or any type of beating that they wished, without hardly making a sound. To only find yourself rocking back and forth sucking on your thumb, crying yourself to sleep or trying to comfort yourself, because that's all that you knew. I remember the very first time I had gotten tied up; I had gotten tied up more than several times and beaten, and for everyone I remember, but my first one, I would have to say, affected me the most, and one that has haunted me the most. I can remember it had been another nice day outside, and as usual we were picking corn out of the field and trying to get apples from the apple tree, fighting over the two seated swings or just running around or getting yelled at by a staff member from doing something they were not fond of. I was approached by the therapist doctor that had seen me the first time and asked if he could borrow me yet again. I had followed him inside and into the same office; he had told me that he was going to be seeing me more to run some tests on me and make sure that I was okay with everything health-wise, and that anything that was going on in the room was not to leave or be told to anyone, not my friends or the staff. He had told me that I needed to take off my shirt and lay down on the couch; at that time, I had only a long shirt that barely covered any of me. I did as he asked and found myself laying down on the couch on my back; he then got out of his chair and walked over to me, sat on the edge of the couch beside me and started to touch my hair and lightly play with my hair.

I had started to squirm around, the fact of anyone touching me was not my thing and something that I did not like. He then proceeded to work his fingers down my face and to check bones. He then moved his hands and started to press around my stomach, and asked if it hurt; I shook my head no. He then started to feel my ribcage and all over my stomach, and did some pokes, and then he stood up and told me that I was done, and that I could put my shirt back on and return outside, and that if anyone asked where I was, I was to tell them that I was with the therapist. I got my shirt on and walked and closed the door. Just as I was getting ready to run and go play outside, I had heard a light scream and yelling, the worst that I could ever hear, but yet faint, almost from another closed room, but it being so far in the back no one in the front would hear it, like I could. Rather than ignoring it and going outside, I went to see what was going on, and if it were someone that I knew. As I got closer to the yelling and screaming and crying, I got in a spot that I could hide enough to see what was going on and what was going to happen. I remember not knowing the kid that well but remember seeing him at times, the outcast, the one that was always getting left out, picked on more than any of us, and abused by the staff more than any of us. We never understood and we never asked why; we just knew how he felt and we dreaded that day when it happened to us. I remember there were three of them; they were dressed up in different clothes to disguise themselves. They had each arm tied up to a pull so tight you could see one side of the arm that was starting to show the bone. At the same time, his other half dangling down from being busted, blisters and so many different colors, his face had blood and cuts all over his lips and face, scars all over. His legs had been so busted up that they were formed in a way I had never seen. It then got silent for one minute, and in that one minute, he looked up with very little breath with blood coming out of his mouth, only to ask, "Why me?" Before you could even think or blink, they took that boy's head with all their force and bashed it into the wall. As his head fell down and more blood was pouring out, they had realized what they had done; they quickly united him and threw his body out of the windows where the dogs were. It had been that any time the staff did not want anyone to know that they killed a child, then they would be fed to the dogs, or be thrown into a ditch and left there to rot. I remember my heart sank, yet I was scared and ran, ran outside back to my friends, hoping that no one saw me and no one would notice that I may have been different or acting different based on what I had just seen.

> "When I become true within myself.. I realize more of who I am and what paths are meant and how they should be followed. When I become true within myself.. I allow more of my guards of fear to come down and learn to understand more of who I can become. When I become true within myself, I learn to fight black shadows of temptations, and crawl my way out of a black hole and into the light of a path that's meant to be but not ignored. When I become true within myself..... I start to believe more than I ever have, courage to fight through even my weakest times and come out with a thankful understanding" (Poem 7).

Sometimes it was hard not talking about some of the things that went on in the orphanage, because if indeed any situations were brought up and the staff found out, they punished you, and they did it in a way that you understood was not okay. I had a best friend in the orphanage; his name is Gabe. He was someone that I felt I could tell anything and never have to worry about, and for the most part, we were always near each other. It had been him I had told that day as to what I had seen and how scared I had been, because I did not want it to happen to me. He had told me that it would have been our secret and that no one would know about it. Little did we know there was someone next to us hiding and had listened to everything that we had said, so then, of course, over a couple of days, the story had come out and it affected everyone, more so me when it came to the time that they found out I had seen and told everything. It had been a day that I would have truly gone and experienced what so many of us went through. We had been in the cages that day, cramped and packed, nothing to do but yell and rock ourselves back and forth, or lay there useless due to the lack of strength and the being beaten, us being treated like lab rats. I had got pulled out buy three different ladies, and while getting pulled out, I was getting beaten for no reason while being dragged along the floor, screaming, knowing what the outcome was going to be, but the more I fought and screamed, the more I got beaten with objects that would pin you right back down to the ground only to cry out in pain, asking for it to stop only to be beaten more to the point where you're lying there, half conscious, because of the beating and being slammed around. Everything had been a mild blur as I was being dragged into a dark hallway, a room that we had heard of but never had seen until now; all we knew was when someone went in, you were lucky if you even came out of that room. There was nothing I could do about it; I had fought every strength that I could and became too weak to even fight back, to even speak or to even move. I was then thrown to the ground to have each arm chained to a wall and my legs tied up to where I could not move or fight back even if I wanted to. As I laid there, barely coherent and blood dripping down my face and arms, I was stripped down to nothing, to be forced with human or dog feces in my mouth and all over my face and body. I was then not only beaten with a whip, but also the wooden stick that they would use one you, thick, it had different shaped holes in there; sometimes they would put nails or certain objects in those holes and beat you with them. I had been beaten with that stock with what felt like shards of glass cutting into my body; every time I was hit by both, I screamed out, and I would get kicked harder in the stomach or side with a foot, or the sticks. I was beaten to the point that I laid there half dead, wishing and praying that it would all be done and that the pain would go away. I don't know what happened that day, but I know someone was watching over me, because I remember that one of the staff said, "We need to let this one go, he has had his punishment for now, I am now done."

It was then that I had walked up and decided to write what I had dreamed of, what had haunted me to not wanting me to go back to sleep because they may come back after me. I had decided that I would only bring up the issues of my nightmares that I felt more comfortable with. There has been a huge part of me that did not trust my therapist, her being a female, because of the way I had been treated by them in the orphanage; my relationship with her and trust were scarce. I had told her that certain dreams from past in the orphanage were coming back, and that it had affected my sleep, the way that I was feeling and thinking, and I was not sure what to do or how to go about it. She had asked if I had been writing theses dreams down; I had lied to her and told her that I had been too scared to write them down, that I did not want to have to think about it, when really I just did not want anyone seeing what I wrote there, and why I had to keep it a secret. We had spent several months working on the issues that I was opened to.

I had arrived at the group home in the summertime, and had school on the campus when the new year started. The school had been in the basement of the house where I was living, so when it was time for me to go to school, I would just walk downstairs. I had to spend a year at this school and prove to them that I could do well in a high school setting, meaning in my grades and also my behavior. Going to public school for me was a treat; it was a way to get out and meet new friends. I had found myself getting involved in 4-H and FFA once I started getting into late middle school, early high. I had always enjoyed animals and became attached to animals every fast. So I then decided that I wanted to raise pigs and heifers, and it was great because the farm that I was living at had them. I started to really get involved, going to rodeos and competitions for showing off my bores and steers. Several years had gone by; I had been working more on the farm and traveling to different states to show off my pigs and the one heifer that I had. I had named her "Meme" (From the Drew Carey show), and at the same time, still going to school. I can still remember those days. It had been a hot summer day; every summer, the group home would have different volunteers to come out and redo their main roads, or any cleaning, or things that needed to be repaired, then they would do it. I had been unloading hay bails off a truck and stacking them into a shed, when I was approached by my counselor and was asked if she could talk to me. I had agreed and followed her in the main house I lived in, and as I walked in, there had been two cops that were in the living room. I had been confused and was not sure what had happened. I was then told that there was some questions that they needed to ask me. I had asked them what it was about and what was going on; I then had been told that I was being accused of sexual foreplay and such on a 12 year old child; at that time, I had been seventeen, my heart sank, and I knew deep down inside it was not true, I was taken inside the house that I was living in and went into the living room where there was the other roommates that had lived there and that had been there to tell their stories. A lot of them had said they did not really know what was going on; others had said things to say things or to get back to me. I had known that I did not do what I was being accused of; after an hour of going around the room and hearing what everyone had to say, I was then taken into the office with my therapist. Once I got in there, I had been viewed back to face with two cops. My heart sank, I had been scared and did not know how to react or what to think; the fear of going to jail was all that was going through my head. I then was told that I was going to be handcuffed and taken to detection. I had started to break down and cry, thinking that it was not fair for something that I did not do. I had been placed in the front of the seat in the cop car rather than the back, he wanted to make sure that I felt safe and that everything was going to be okay. He had tried to talk to me on the way down, but all I could do was either sit there in silence and nod my head, or say nothing at all. I had no clue what to expect or what the outcome of this would be.

> "Today I learned more of myself and my mistakes. Today I learned more of my feelings and how I could overcome them each moment, not in fear but in courage. Today I learned to express hate and turn it into thankfulness, and the joy I got to experience. Today I say thank you for the emotions you brought my way. It made me a stronger person inside. Today I say thank you for the love that you gave me, it built more courage inside. Today I say thank you for the tears we shared together, it brought the best of who and what I am I can become. Today... I say thank you for letting me take my mask off my face more and more each day to be

able to feel and experience more of what I'm to become" (poem 8).

I had arrived in the afternoon; I remember because I was told that they were just serving lunch and that I was going to get a tray if I had wanted one. I nodded my head yes and sat there in silence, I had gone there for the booking, where I was asked what seemed like endless questions to things I had no clue to or no understanding of my life. I had changed into their jail clothes. I was put into a youth correctional system, a jail for youths who could not be responsible or could just not obey the law, so that's where they were sent until they did their time. I had been told that I was going to have a cell to myself, because what I got charged with, I was to be kept safe from people hurting or what not, which I did not mind, but night after night of being alone and in a small cell left me to flashbacks of the orphanage and what it was like to be locked in the cages, dreams that had me waken in cold sweats to only want to be held and told it was going to be okay, instead to wake up alone in a cell and dark, and no one to talk. It had only been less than a week that I was moved into a different place. I had my own room yet again, but my behavior was based on levels and scores, so if I did what I was supposed to do that day or go above, then we were rewarded with snakes, or we stayed up later. I had seemed to like it, but my room that I had been in was what gave me even more nightmares, the room just did not feel right, I always hated going to sleep in it. There had been a night that I was led into a long-lost dream that I had wished it did not haunt. You see in the dream...

It had been those dreams that kept me from wanting to sleep; it had been those dreams that I did not want to have to relive and instead I did everything to block out those thoughts that built more and more anger each time, and every time that the bad nightmares came, more walls would be built inside me, where feelings could not be felt and love could not be expressed but to only be left in numbness and confusions of lost answers. My adopted parents had moved to Utah at the time; my adopted father got a job offer in Utah and decided to pack up and his family and go live a new life. I had seen my adopted father a couple of times, but the person that had surprised me and stuck by my side to make sure that I was going to get out of there as soon as possible was my adopted mother; she fought with the courts and did what she needed to do in order for me to be out of where I was. They had also known that I was not that kind of person, nor would I had done it. Several months had gone buy and I was finally told that I could go home. I had been very excited yet very scared because I was not sure what to expect being back with my adopted parents and living with them in the same house after nearly seven years. It had been my adopted mother and I that flew back to Utah and were greeted by some of the family members there to pick us up and take us home. I was surprised with more of the positive feedback that I had gotten rather than negative. I had for sure thought that I was going to be looked at differently and that I would be teased about it, and instead it was hardly ever brought up and we went our ways as if nothing had ever happened. My summer had been spent working and spending time with my cousins or hanging out with friends. This had started to go well until I had gone back into high school. You see, when I had come to Utah one of the requirements I had to do and take was a class to make sure that I was not a threat to myself or younger children; after nearly several months of treatments, I was found that I was not a threat and my case was dismissed. In the meantime, I was seeing a therapist for my behavior problems and my mood swings. I was then given certain medication for my troubled sleeping, anxiety, and depression. Witch there had been times that the pills that I was on had made me feel very suicidal, but then I had had the problem of suicide at the age of twelfth, so it was something for me that was very hard to take control. When school started up again, I had been in high school and had got involved with the wrong crowd I wanted to be accepted; that had been who and what I was all that I could remembered, so there had been a girl that I had gotten to know and a couple of guys, and we would ditch some class and go smoke cigs or go smoke weed. Around that time, I had not known really about pills and what they were worth. I had been asked by the girl one day if I took pills and what they were. She had told me that she would love me forever and that she thought I would be the best if I had brought some of those pills and that she would feel better.

When bedtime came around, that's the thing we all dreaded and never looked forward to. The staff would put on white sheets that covered them from head to toe with two holes in the sheet where they could see where they were going; in our mind we believed that they were bad ghost because they came around and made sure you were silent and asleep, and if you were not any of those, then they would punish you until you were forced to sleep, so even if you could not sleep, it was closing your eyes and pretending that you were asleep. Sometimes the ones that were forced to be put to sleep would not wake up the next morning; there was nothing they could do about it. Each side of their arms were tied, and each side of their feet were tied and beaten in ways you could not imagine, to only hear the bloody scream of a child and only to be forced to watch. We knew what it meant when the body would be thrown out of the back window. There was a night that I can remember very clearly.

It had been a restless night. The moon was bright, the hole inside of the building was lit. Nights by the moon's reflections and the shadows were covered in dark spots. You could hear the sound of crickets and dogs barking, some children sleeping, others whispering so lightly you could hardly hear what the conversation itself was. I had laid there for what seemed to be quite a while. The staff had already come through twice and had already done their night inspections. I then decided to get out of bed and make my way downstairs, as I slowly creeped my way down the stars to make sure not to hit the creaking sounds in the floorboards. As I got closer down the the bottom, I stopped and grasped the handle railing to look in between, and seeing two lady staff taking off the ghost sheets and putting them back on laughing at the same time. While still scared, I had decided to go back to my bed as quickly and quietly before they saw me and caught me. We did not know that they were people dressed in sheets; we had believed and were told that they were ghosts indeed, and that if we did not sleep, they would come in the middle of the night and take us and beat us. The thought of ever going to sleep was impossible, being scared to even going to sleep, laying there chained or tied up where you could not move as much, or were beaten to the point that even the thought of moving; it was a feeling of wanting to, rather, wanting to give up and not fight anymore, wondering what the next day would bring, and if that cries and prayers were heard, to be adopted by an American family. There had been many experiments that were done not only on me, but the rest that were in there, some that you still hear about now throughout many countries, of children being forced to have sex with one another as they're being watched and told what to do, but in the most disturbing way that you could think of, having objects involved and being beaten at the same time, only to have laughter heard from the staff. They had made us try sexual experiments with different animals or one on one with the staff.

At the same time and always being treated like animals, we were being whipped. They say that God works in mysterious ways, and sometimes we don't have a full understanding of the meaning and why, but they happen. There was only one really good memory that I had while I was in the orphanage. I could not tell you who this person was, more of who this older lady had been that came to see me one to two times a month for an hour each time. I can't tell you the detail of her, and what see looked like or even the scent of her smell, but I can tell you that she at the time had been in her late fifties or sixties. I could tell you that when I was around this person, I felt very safe, peaceful, and calm inside me, as if nothing bad could ever happen to me. That was the best thing, because for that one hour, I knew that I could not be hurt but loved the way I should have.

She had brought me food every time. She had a brown hand-woven handled box that she would take food out of; it was not very much but enough that we could both eat and enjoy ourselves. Those were my happy moments in the orphanage, the moments I looked forward to, and more than anything, I think those were the moments that kept me alive. Then one day, she stopped coming. I did not know why or have the understanding, but only to think that it was me and that they stopped caring. Each month that went by and I did not get to see her, a piece of me died more and more inside of me. I had started to get to the point where I had stopped fighting for something that I wanted, that any of those children wanted, the love and bonding. I had had it to only lose it. When different parents came through to the orphanage, we were always told about it before they came, and how we needed to be on our best behavior, and the ones that they thought were good enough to show, they would dress them in nice clothes and make it look like they were getting treated well. And when they arrived, all the children would run up to the parents that were looking to adopted, to only have children running up grabbing onto them, begging them to take them to America with them and that they no longer wanted to be where they were. There were also children that did not come running up and trying the same thing. Some had given up on the fact that they were not going to get adopted, so they were the ones that were secluded in the back; others were handicapped or beaten or tied up to the point where they could not move.

I was left there for four days, in the dark, cold. No food and very little water. Four days that felt like a week, four days that I had experiments done to me. Things that still haunt me. The first day that I had was beaten and forced to eat feces. I was left alone for the rest of the night after I was cleaned off the best they could. The second day, the therapist came in with one of the ladies, untied my hands, and told me that I needed to go with the therapist. I went with him and went into the same office; he had told me to lay on the couch. He then locked the door and sat on the edge of the couch. I laid there with still some blood all over my body, still too weak to barely move. I laid there as he then started to take his hands and run them down my body and started working towards my private where he then started to fondle and play with it. I had reacted by pulling his hands away. I had felt uncomfortable; he then looked at me and backhanded me, telling me that he was in charge, and what he said went, and that I was to do it with no questions asked, or the consequences would be worse. He then started to fondle me again. I did not want to be hit again, so I let him play with it. He then started to unzip his zipper to his slacks, and he had pulled his out, and had told me to touch it. I had refused the first time, only getting hit harder than the first time, so then I followed his demand until he then asked me to put my mouth around it. I then refused and fought back to the point where I was beaten to the point where I could no longer fight back; he had forced me to suck him. And then to have a cloth put in my mouth so no one could hear me while he turned me around and had his way with me. I laid there in more pain than I had ever been.

I had laid there only to see more blood that I had been covered in. He had also seen that his member was covered in blood and his pants, which made him even more upset, so he beat me, and made me do the same things that he demanded the first time. After he was done, he had left me there hopeless on the ground as he went into a bag and got a new change of clothes and put them on as nothing ever happened, and then opened the door and called to the staff, claiming that I had fallen and hurt myself, causing blood to come out. I was dragged out of the room and put back into the same dark room, and each arm was tied harder every time, almost if not feeling my bones. As I laid there with my head down to have blood dripping out of my mouth and nose and from the side of my face, I was beaten more to the point that my yelling and cries faded every time, only to be knocked unconscious. The staff would have competitions of who could do more damage to a youth's arm, whether it was chaining their wrist up, or with ropes, whatever they could find to tie you up and cause the most damage is what they got the thrill out of. All I remember is the three days that felt like a week were one of the most disturbing memories that still flashes in my mind more than usual, leaving me restless with sleepless nights. Several weeks had gone by. I had learned to not say anything and that it was best to shut my mouth, I had even excluded talking to my best friend which was very hard for me.

The enemy would leave you alone if you were not a major threat. He/she would not bother you if you didn't have something amazing in your future. Focus on you, your love you have to give. Don't worry about any "online" haters; that's just silly. Let them do their job. To be unhappy, jealous, and ugly. Take the high road, be enlightened, and stay strong in spirit.

DON'T miss the
opportunities to
make a difference
everyday, touch
someones heart,
encourage a mind
and lead someone
to become what
they aspire to be... Reyna Angelica Reyes (Poem 9)

I could not tell you how long it was that I was in detention for; all I knew was that it had been my first time. I had been freaked out and unsure what to think or react, at times feeling numb and alone. I was being accused of sexual things on someone younger than me. Had I become a monster? And why was I being punished for something that I did not do?

I was upset where I had been, and I knew that I did not belong where I was. It did not make it any better because there were some other youths that were in with me that had been in the group home as well at one point, and I did not even care for them, even when I was in the group home. After some months and going through court, I had my adopted parents by my side, more of my adopted mother. At that time, my adopted father had a job in Utah at the Hill Airforce Base. That would have required my adopted family to move. What that had meant to me and for me was something that shocked me and something that I did not accept.

I had been told by my adopted mother that once I was released, we would take a flight to Utah and that I would be living with them under their home and that they wanted to make a family work again. Guess you could say more of a new, fresh start. I remember that there had been a part of me that had felt a little excited, but more nervous of what was going to happen, and if this were going to work. As for the therapy sessions that we had throughout the years, some worked, and others did not. I still found myself going to a therapist, even when I had to move to Utah. You see, one of the requirements from the courts was that I had to take a sex class to make sure that I was not threat to little children or better yet, "a child pedophile." I remember going to the classes. I knew that this was not me, and some of the other youths my age made me feel very uncomfortable at times. But in order to complete it, I had to go to the classes and one on one with a therapist, which went on for a little over a year until I was not considered a threat to young youths.

Living with my adopted parents for the first year and being back with them, I went back to old habits. I got into arguments with my parents and did sneaky activities, and of course, my lying was not any better. I had started to pick up smoking cigarettes; I was in high school at the time. I found that smoking felt like a stress relief, and at the time, was my only comfort when I needed it. It did not take too long for my adopted father to find out.

I had used the excuse that I was going on walks. I always thought that was the best way to go smoke and sneak, but what I always forgot about was the smell, so my adopted parents where dumb. The only thing that came out of my adopted father when he caught me was, "I can't stop you from smoking cigarettes, it's your health, just smoke near the house." I remembered that I had a hard time sleeping. That was the first thing that I had to move back in with my adopted parents. There had been a lot of stress on my end, and I felt as though I always had to walk on eggshells and felt I never could be myself.

In my own house, even when I was just being me, I think it was more a fear messing up and how my adopted father was going to accept me. I came to fear my own adopted father. Inside it killed me; he was someone that at one point I could all my best friend and hero, and the more it seemed that I could be myself around him, more of me died inside.

I had a restless night being back in a house with my adopted parents. It had been more than five years since I had lived with them and still much communication when I was in the group home in Colorado. And when I did sleep, they were restless nights of flashbacks and memories of my orphanage and the day I found out that an American family was going to adopt me.

You see, at the point that I was in the process of being adopted, I was placed in the hospital. I had become sick, and I was pretty much shutting down. I had remembered the first time I had met and seen my adopted parents; I was very excited yet nervous. I had become more excited when I had seen that they had brought me toys, and toys were something that I had always wanted and had dreamed of.

I can't tell you how long I was in the hospital for, but I can tell you that I remember the day that I was getting to leave to the United States with my new adopted parents to start a new life. They had bought me new clothes and hats and shoes, things that we had about, and my dream of owning my own pair of clothes is what had excited me. Leaving my best friends and the one that I had become close to were the hardest things to let go off. I wanted to bring my friend with me, and knowing that I could not is what killed me the most inside, and I knew it would have been my last time seeing them.

After nearly seven years, I was finally saying goodbye to a place that I would never miss and never would wish anyone to even have to experience what I had to go through, but at the same time, I knew that the memories were going to haunt me for the rest of my life. The secret within will eventually get the best of us and eventually memories that become secrets will come out.

When you let your emotions get the best of you, you lose what and who you are. Don't frown on the emotions, but smile on them because it makes you a better and stronger person. How we choose to Handle our emotions is what we become tomorrow. Fight with courage and not fear, cry your tears and experience the hurt and smile upon the memories that affect you in order to really find the true you and what is meant for you and your life" (poem 10).

> "When we learn to stop fighting, when we learn to stop
> the fears, the anger and the hate. We start to feel more
> of who and what we are. We learn what it is that we
> want, what we can and can't accept in our lives. Even
> if it's letting go of the things that once meant some-
> thing to our lives. When we learn to breathe out the

toxic substances of negativity and breathe in the better side of life.. Then we have the strength and power beyond our wildest dreams to achieve the unknown and make it ours" (Poem 10).

"To the voices that said I could not. To the voices that said I could not amount to anything. To the voices that said I let fear get the best of me and who I am.. I thank you for the voices that gave me the courage to fight my battles, overcome the fears and to not steer away from open doors and paths presented to me and my life. Without the voices.. I would not be standing stronger and fighting even more to make a change in my life and become more complete as to what my journeys are and meant" (Poem 11).

"When we learn to let go.. We learn to accept, and when we learn to accept, we learn to feel more and understand the paths that are meant. We learn to experience the past but learn from them to know what we can and do in our lives. With courage, we become one and become one... We have the power at the grips of our hands" (Poem 12).

"If u love your child the way you say u do, support and love them no matter what with no judgment . Be there for them and not give up because it was too hard for you. The child is not the failure, it's you as a parent that failed because you did not have the confidence or the faith to make it work and you let your pride get the best of who and what you are. Life is too short and you get to decide what really matters to you and your life, and when that is no longer there... Guess who that really lies on?" (Poem 13).

"When I find myself.. I face fear with courage. When I learn to fight my own battles, I fight with the strengths that are provided to my life. When I learn to accept the terms of reality... I Discover more of what I can offer not only to myself.. But those around me with open arms and a kind heart" (Poem 14).

"I can't keep chasing something that's not there, I can't keep chasing something that is not given back, know matter how hard I have tried and the Sacrifices I've made when you want nothing in return.. So with my love, I'm setting you free and wishing the best in whatever the paths are presented to you and your paths" (Poem 15).

"My love of fire will never die inside for what we had and what it could have been, but now you see it's time for me to spread my wings and fly away and experience my journey and what's meant for me and my life and what matters to me" (Poem 16).

"When we stop the fears, when we stop the stress, when we stop the what if's and how we feel our life should pand out. And turn things over to a higher power and truly let go with the understanding of what faith is. You would be surprised what lands in our lives and the choices of paths and doors we get to walk through and on" (Poem 17).

"Today I felt, today I cried, today I let the best of me be affected in every way. Today I concurred with my anger, my sadness and my tears. I thanked God for allowing me to have the people in my life that he has presented to me at one point or another.. Some still in my life and others that have gone home. Today I reflected and thanked that I got to feel and experience the joy and love. Because without the journeys that come and go through my paths.. I would not be where I am today" (Poem 18).

"Remember to not let the best of our affections and emotions get to you from the past.. Learn to love it. Learn to embrace what it was and where you are in your life today. The choices we let affect us, is then what we and who we are tomorrow" (Poem 19).

"When I touch.. Do u feel my wrath back.. When I kiss you so gently.. Does our world stop? Do u lose all track of who you are and do your worries stop. When I tell you that my heart still beats for you more than I could ever have imagined, do you believe? Do you feel? Does the fear pass away? When I tell you forever is what I have dreamed.. Do you know what a lifetime I want?" (Poem 20).

"When I hold you.. Does forever become realistic every time, and do the voices made since when I say.. " I'm keeping you forever and for always. To grow old and never hurt. To never hide my fears but to have an open mind and. Better understanding and not to give up.. Even threw our worst battles.. If love is what's meant to be.. Then our love will unite as one when the time is presented" (Poem 20).

"Our thoughts of thinking and having an open mind is like an umbrella, when it opens... Anything is possible" (Poem 21).

"It was fear that made me who I am.. It was facing the past that made me become stronger in who I am. It was my pride that let the best of my world get to me to be faced with new challenges in my life. It was the people that told me I amounted to something. A path that I needed to discover and believe in" (Poem 22).

"We are who we are.. The power to become every aspect of what we feel and what we want all lies in honesty. Faith and courage is a path of fears unless we take the mask off and walk the path that's meant and not denial" (Poem 23).

"The enemy would leave you alone if you were not a major threat. He/She would not bother you if you didn't have something amazing in your future. Focus on you, your love you have to give. Don't worry about any "online" haters, that's just silly. Let them do their job. To be unhappy, jealous and ugly. Take the high road, be enlightened and stay strong in spirit.
DON'T miss the
opportunities to
make a difference
everyday, touch
someones heart,
encourage a mind
and lead someone
to become what
they aspire to be...Reyna Angelica Reyes" (Poem 24).

"Today I learned more of myself and my mistakes. Today I learned more of my feelings and how I could overcome them each moment, not in fear but in courage. Today I learned to express hate and turn it into thankfulness, and the joy I got to experience. Today I say thank you for the emotions you brought my way. It made me a stronger person inside. Today I say thank you for the love that you gave me, it built more courage inside. Today I say thank you for the tears we shared together, it brought the best of who and what I am I can become. Today... I say thank you for letting me take my mask off my face more and more each day to be able to feel and experience more of what I'm to become" (Poem 25).

"All I ever wanted was to show you what I can offer and give to you. All I ever wanted was to take away the fear and hurt and bring back the spark of joy we once knew and grew to love. All I ever wanted was to bring wishing stars into your life and make dreams turn into reality. All I ever wanted was your happiness in whatever that may be. I give my love, for you to find your paths and the journeys you will experience and go through. My love for you is like a candle.. It lights for you to throw your weakest times. My love will never stop fighting nor beating" (Poem 26).

"Some say paths are meant to be the way it is. Based on fear and letting the best get to us. Me... I fight my battles, conquer my fears and keep the best of me on the paths that's presented." Cheers to a new day and endless possibilities...." (Poem 27).

"When I become true within myself.. I realize more of who I am and what paths are meant and how they should be followed. When I become true within my-self.. I allow more of my guards of fear to come down and learn to understand more of who I can become. When I become true within myself, I learn to fight black shadows of temptations, and crawl my way out of a black hole and into the light of a path that's meant to be but not ignored. When I become true within my-self..... I start to believe more than I ever have, courage to fight through even my weakest times and come out with a thankful understanding" (Poem 28).

"It was your love that forced me to make a better person inside me, it was your love that made me want to work more towards my goals and dreams. It was your love that had me believe that having a family would be worth the fight. It was your love that made me feel all over again, to find my true self being and to experience life that we fought for. It was your love that made me more free inside then I could ever have imagined. I looked at a brighter tomorrow and let go" (Poem 29).

"Today I say thank you to the voices that were heard. Today I say thank you for allowing me to experience the paths and choices of today's accomplishments. Today I say thank you for allowing me to see what life is really meant for and not have to hide the better me. Today I say thank you for giving me the freedom to speak out, the freedom for fighting. To be able to experience my own battles and struggles in order to make myself stronger and better in my life" (Poem 30).

"When I tell you I love you, do you feel my heart beat at the same time? When I tell you I love you, do you feel the passion more and more each time? When I tell you I love you, does my touch get you lost ? Do your thoughts melt and do you get lost in unexplained emotions, but only in silent tears because you felt more and more each time. When I tell you I love you,.. Do you believe me when I tell you you're gorgeous? And does it make you want more? When I tell you I love you... Love is what I mean, with every beat of my heart, with every emotion we get to experience together" (Poem 31).

"Today I cried my battles, today I fought my battles and learned to become one. I reached out as far as the universe allowed me. To become stronger for me and the path that lies in front of me. I concurred the paths and climbed to the top and reached a purpose.. A purpose to become my own self" (Poem 32).

"Relationships may not make sense at times, and how love has a way of towing with every emotion that we have. When we get to actually experience feelings, and thoughts that can't be expressed but only in joy of tears. Then will you have had the true understanding, and how it's meant" (Poem 33).

"Cherish the arguments, the hurt, the tears and the other emotions that come and play, because without those in our lives... Then how was love to be explained and how were emotions to be expressed and most of all.. What would that make us?" (Poem 34).

"Don't forget who you are, don't forget the paths that were set and meant. Don't forget to let the best of your world be affected by fears, anger, hate and hurt. Instead walk through doors and paths with every emotion you have. To experience, to understand and acknowledge life. Fight your fears, accomplish your battles and smile at a new beginning" (Poem 35).

"When will my heart beat be heard and felt? When will my touch ease your pain and grow into a warmth of love? When will my kiss melt your thoughts away and feel every emotion of who I am and what I can offer? When will my "I love you" be missed when you need them the most?. When you grab my hand do you feel my love back? When you kiss me, do you melt your thoughts away and feel safe in my arms at the same time? ..When did fantasy's turn into illusion's? And when did illusions become reality? To impossible endless wonders of worlds and the true meaning of life itself. The battles I fight today are the ones I will achieve Tomorrow and stand up more for who I am, for a better me and a better tomorrow" (Poem 36).

"When we grasp at the universe and learn to let go of the fears, the what if's... Imagine what we can be capable of and how far we can go.. Reach and feel the burn to the destination that's meant to be, not what we think it should be" (Poem 37).

"The path to our destination is like music in our lives, it impacts us and who we are. We feel the music, we understand the words and the meaning of what the music sings to us and how we embrace it. The path to our destination... is like music... How far are you willing to go? "Never forget who you are and what your path of destiny is. Life may not make sense. Breathe it, feel it and embrace the better understanding of life. But never ignore a knock on a door that is presented in your life" (Poem 38).

"Today I became the best.. Today I fought to fight my battles and make myself stronger. Today I reflected on the past, not in fear but a better way of understanding my paths and what I can overcome. Today I say thank you for letting me experience the fear, the hurt, and the anger, because without those in my life.. "Who would I become, and what journeys lie in the path of my destiny" Today, I make a pledge to become a better person inside and not let outside drama get the best of my world, but to stay on the right path and into the light of happiness and courage. Today, I allow myself to never hide who I am, but to express love and hope to those around me" (Poem 39).

"Remember this, when life may have you down and ur at a road of feeling overwhelmed... Stop... Breath and remember the blessing that has already been provided for you in your life.. They may not be what you want at the time.. But in time with time things will present when it's least expected" (Poem 40).

"Lesson to the beat of my heart, lesson to the voice that speaks out and what it's telling you. Take my hand and walk with me in faith and courage and not of fear. Reach for the sky and catch each star making a dream and holding them dear to only making them become more real. Reach for the moon to guide through dark times, and not to lose the best of who u can become. Make me a bird, so that I may fly.. far, far way, to expand my wings and to experience life that is meant to be and not the way I feel best fit. Release me of my fears and bring journeys of endless possibilities in my life" (Poem 41).

"When I stop fighting my battles, I then have the understanding of what fear is and what it takes to make myself stronger. Today, I face my battles with courage and a better understanding of what is meant to be. Today.. Becomes a new battle of courage and an open mind to a new beginning" (Poem 42).

"Dear God,
Today I give thanks, to allowing another day to be able to experience the better side of who and what I can become each day, to walk forward with faith and courage and not to look back in fear, but to look back and learn from my experiences and to become more understanding of the paths and doors that are presented in my life. Today I say thank you, for allowing me to be faced with many years of battles and to be able to take the mask off my face by throwing away the past and walking to the better side of endless possibilities to not only a better me, but a better tomorrow" (Poem 43).

"If I spoke out to you.. Would you care about the lesson and understand my thoughts? If I spoke out and told you what you were doing to me and others.. Would you care about the lesson and understand my cries? If I spoke out to you and told you that the feeling of being alone and not wanted, affected the cuts to take away the pain.. Would you be there to hold my hand and tell me it was going to be ok?.." (Poem 44).

"When I become strong within myself... I learn to express the better side of who I want to be And not how others see me best fit in their world. When I become strong within myself... I stop allowing bullying in my life and stand for what's right and what I believe in. When I become strong within myself... I stop lying to myself and the people out there that mean the most to me, to take off the mask and show others who and what I can achieve in my life. When I become strong with myself.... I stop trying to force and take control over things that have no matter or are not time to be presented in my life. When I become strong within myself.. I give more thanks to myself and the people around me that believed in what they saw in me" (Poem 45).

"Today I embrace the here and now.. To not ignore, but to take lessons and to have a better understanding of my life and what I'm meant to be. Today I embrace my most inner weakness to not let it over power my life.. But to embrace most inner peace in me, to find my faith and courage. Today I embrace love in my life and release the toxins of unknown dark paths. Today I embrace my feelings and stand up more for who I am and what I know I can become. Today... I say thank you.. Thank you for another day to be faced with trials, emotions, and the decisions of right and wrongs, leaving us to become more within ourselves" (Poem 46).

"Looking at past memories can either break us or end up making us strong each and every time we realize.. That when we have no control over things, places and people... Then we realize the true definition of forgiveness and turn the rest to the universe knowing that what plays in our lives and the paths that are being presented in our life's are then what's meant to be" (Poem 47).

"Dear God,

 I thank you for the strength you gave me to become stronger in my moments of weakness at times being faced with unknown decisions. I thank you for allowing tears to not be expressed of sadness but the tears of courage and strength. Today I thank you for not letting temptations get the best of who i am but instead embrace 1225 courage and faith allowing to stay focused on a path of endless opportunities in my life, and not paths of spiering illusions of webs, but to embrace each second and moment I have in my life. Dear God... I thank you for the strength you gave me to become stronger in my most weakest moments and allowing me to become stronger within myself and what I can become. Dear God, make me a bird.. So that I may expand my wings and fly into the sunset and let dreams become endless possibilities" (Poem 48)"

"Today,.. I live for a better side of me and what I can become today. Today I walk in the paths of the now and not the illusions of yesterday's past. Today, I become forgiving and understanding to an open mind of accepting the paths presented in my life. "Today I say thank you for yet another beautiful day in my life to be able to still get to continue to fly and experience" (Poem 49).

"Dear God,
Today I give thanks for letting me experience the better side of who I am today and what more I can become

tomorrow. Today I give thanks to the support that surrounds my everyday struggles and the faith to walk on a better path of tomorrow and not steer to paths of illusions but the paths of faith and courage to endless possibilities. Today I give thanks for the joy in my life and not the past of yesterday's sorrowful memories. Today I give thanks for giving me wings to fly, to experience, to feel and to understand the better side of not only me.. but the path of what is meant to be" (Poem 50).

"Don't let others tell you, you can't be someone else, fight for what you want to become and not what others think you should become..." (Poem 51).

"Sometimes old habits re enter our life's, leaving us at a blank of not knowing why or not having the understanding of the manner in itself. Embrace the understanding and take control of the issue in itself, how you chose to take control of your journey today... is then what you become tomorrow. "Sometimes the things we need to hear may not always settle well within our feelings and how to choose to handle the situation. Rather than being affected by the situation, embrace the understanding of the outcome" (Poem 52).

"Life's decisions are the paths we make and choose along the way, sometimes good and sometimes bad, others having a true understanding of the paths we were on and others leaving us at a dead end at times to only leaving us at not having a full understanding of who we are or can become. We sometimes let our pride and emotions get the best of us, some to only hide away from the world because they are told they will never amount to anything nor themselves to be left with scars of endless tears of emotions. We learn to fight our own battles to discover what our meaning is to life and who we really are. It's then that when we get to feel, we express, and when we express not only are voices heard, but then we become more free within ourselves" (Poem 53).

"Sometimes the path choices that we have taken or have been presented in our life's may not always make since and we may not always have a better understanding of the outcome of itself, but throughout the years I have learned as hard as life may get, and as much as we may want to give up all hope within who we can become and who we are, I smiled on the experiences, not because what I had to go through, but the tools and the experiences that I can can share and become someone that I am meant to be and not what the world should see me" (Poem 54).

"Always remember to not let past memories and secrets affect who you are and what you become, when the mask comes off and you get to show the true being of who you are, then will you become free within yourself and experience feeling and discovering who you are and what you can offer to yourself and the world itself, remember to not let fears get the best of your world but to walk in faith on a better and new path to the, "Yellow Brick Road" to endless possibilities to discovering our true paths of happiness" (Poem 55).

"Letting past memories and secrets affect the best of who we are, are paths of webs to self destruction, wearing a mask to be someone you're not meant to be, are illusions and fantasies that then themselves turned into lost hopes. Don't let the best of you be affected by things that can not be controlled, life may not make sense, in the meantime, always remember to smile back at the curve balls thrown your way and to never frown from the path of open doors to endless paths of opportunity" (Poem 56).

"My words can't express the joy and warmth of unexplained feelings that I have, but knowing the feeling that I have in me is more than I have ever felt in my life and a feeling that once was a lost dream to only be found upon a wishing star. My love I place my heart into your hands to cherish and to never forget but to hold and embrace every beat I have for you" (Poem 57).

"My love takes my hands and flies with me upon endless wishing stars and makes illusions become endless possibilities, possibilities that then become our reality. Take my hand and dance with me to feel every beat and rhythm while we experience endless wonders of our love into vast unknown worlds to cherish and never forget but to embrace the joy, laughter, and the memories we will get to experience together. My love, words can't express the joy and warmth of unexplained vast of emotions that I hold, a feeling that I would never lose nor forget but to embrace to the fullest and to never forget. I am often told more than once how I'm a mysterious person.. And my reply then becomes.. Welcome to endless possibilities where mysterious then become reality" (Poem 58).

"Don't let people, places and things get the best of your world, be proud and stand up and fight for who and what you are. Wearing a mask makes you weak, being your true inner self is just a stepping stone to being the person you're meant to be, not what others think you should be labeled as." Never be scared to express your thoughts and your feelings, stand up and fight for who and what you can become, embrace today and let yesterday go as it is done and over with, don't let tomorrow's worries get the best of your emotions for it has not arrived. Live and breathe for today and enjoy and embrace it to the fullest as if it was your last" (Poem 59).

"Let today's voices be spoken, let today's voices be heard and understood. Let today's thoughts turn into endless illusions to then be endless reality and mythical dreams to be turned into endless possibilities to a better and new start" (Poem 60).

Born in Romania, Ian Goehring spent from birth to age seven in an orphanage, being adopted by an American family, coming to the U.S. in 1991, living with them for about six years, and then with the state and foster care until the age of 19 years old. Goehring is a recovering drug addict, and started a nonprofit organization not only to give back to Romania, but also those who need a lending hand.